List
Building
Blueprint

How to Generate 100+ Leads
Per Day for Any Business

Chris King

Disclaimer

This book has been written for information purposes only. Every effort has been made to make this Book as complete and accurate as possible. However, there may be mistakes in typography or content. Also, this book provides information only up to the publishing date. Therefore, this Book should be used as a guide - not as the ultimate source.

The purpose of this Book is to educate. The author and the publisher does not warrant that the information contained in this book is fully complete and shall not be responsible for any errors or omissions. The author and publisher shall have neither liability nor responsibility to any person or entity with respect to any loss

or damage caused or alleged to be caused
directly or indirectly by this book.

Table of Contents

List Building and Its Benefits

If you have a small business, are doing online marketing, or simply have a specialized interest or hobby and would like to interact with others who share your passion, you need to have an email list. That's because email remains the single most effective way to connect with other people online.

Unlike instant messaging or video chatting, email doesn't require you to be constantly online or monitoring your smart phone or portable device. Unlike social media, email doesn't need daily updating in order to remain relevant. Unlike direct mail or traditional marketing, email doesn't cost a fortune nor does it require you to devote a lot of time and labor to make it be effective.

Instead, building your list of email contacts and using that list to promote your products, services or ideas is still the easiest, most cost-effective and most user-friendly ways to connect with a large group of prospective customers, clients or fans.

Despite critics who claim that email is being replaced with other, faster methods of online interaction – such as instant messaging, Twitter, or even SnapChat – the fact remains that most Internet users have at least one email account that they monitor regularly.

Need proof that email remains relevant? Answer this question: Have you checked your email anytime in the past 48 hours? If so, then you already know how important email remains to the average Internet user.

List Building Essentials

Building a large email list is the starting point to whatever Internet marketing program you have in mind. When you have a list of hundreds or even thousands of contacts, you can expect a certain percentage of people to respond to any single email you send out promoting a product, service, or even a link to a blog or other relevant content.

So building your list by attracting people who are interested in the types of products or services you promote, or share your passion for a particular interest, is essential to the success of your online marketing strategy. Once you have a list of loyal customers, contacts or followers, you can promote an endless supply of niche-related products, services or links in order to drive response.

When you continually add new people to your list, you can create an effective sales funnel that can earn you profits.

There are both free and paid ways to add people to your list. If you are starting out with a low marketing budget – or no marketing budget – you need not worry. You can start with free list-building techniques and after you start to make money with your list, you can reinvest a portion of your revenues into paid list-building techniques so you can make even more sales and keep making money indefinitely.

If you already have at least one email account, you probably are familiar with what an email list is and how it works. But building a large list – anywhere from 100 to 10,000 contacts or more – requires a little more administrative skill, management time and organization than the ordinary Gmail or Yahoo email account holder possesses.

To manage a list that large, you need some help in the form of an autoresponder. This is software that you buy that takes care of most of the tedious administrative tasks that come with managing your list, such as sending out emails according to a pre-established schedule, collecting email addresses of new subscribers, distributing your free giveaways, directing traffic to the appropriate sales pages and other promotional links, and so on.

Your autoresponder also will provide you with valuable data that you can use to better manage your online business, such as how many people actually click through from the emails you send out, which users always delete your emails without reading them, even how long the average user spends reading your emails before clicking off. You can use data like this to fine tune your email promotions so that they are more surgical and connect more effectively with a larger percentage of your list.

While there are dozens of autoresponders out there that you can get, there are three that offer the best array of services at the most affordable prices:

- Aweber

- GetResponse

- PureLeverage

Getting a high-quality autoresponder is sort of like being a business owner who hires a hard-working, efficient and honest manager to run the day-to-day operations for you. Once you give the autoresponder the general directions you want, it can easily and effectively handle most of the time-consuming administrative duties automatically, so you can focus on the larger "big picture" issues related to running your business.

Squeeze Pages and Their Uses

The fastest way to build your list is to give away something valuable for free that people interested in the types of products, services or interests you are promoting will find irresistible.

For example, if you specialize in weight loss products, you could offer a free video that explains the "Top 10 Ways to Lose 30 Pounds in 30 Days". If you are promoting golf getaway vacations, you could give away a free 30-minute online consultation with a golf pro. Or if your goal is to create a forum in which literature fans can interact with each other, you could offer a list of the top 100 Great Books.

The free giveaway is called the Lead Magnet Report (LMR) or a lead magnet because it works the same way a polarized magnet does: It attracts people to join your list by providing them with some sort of high-value content in exchange for their email address.

Once you capture their email address, you can then use it to send an endless series of emails promoting your products, services, links to relevant content or whatever you want. You also can provide a continual supply of even more free high-value content in order to nurture your relationship with you contacts. If your subscribers know they are going to get something that they are interested in and will find whenever they receive an email from you, they will be more likely to open your emails, or at least not delete them without reading them.

Content Creation

Now that you have an autoresponder and understand the importance of having a high-value lead magnet, the next step is to create your free giveaway so you can offer it on your squeeze page to build your list.

There are two basic ways to develop a great lead magnet that people who are interested in your niche will want: Develop it yourself or use content that already exists.

Figure 1 - Example of a Squeeze Page

If you are skilled at writing, creating original video or recording audio courses, you might consider developing your own content, especially if you are already knowledgeable and passionate about your niche. If you can create a short report, make a brief instructional video, record a useful MP3, or even lead an online webinar, you can save yourself the expense and trouble of having somebody else create content for you or buying existing content.

The original content you create doesn't have to be long or involved, as long as it is something your subscribers or potential subscribers will want or can use in their everyday lives. It can be a simple 10-page short report or a brief 5-minute video shot using your laptop's built-in video camera in which you explain how to perform some task or explain some idea.

Another option is to hire a freelancer to create original content for you. If you have an idea for a short report, video or audio recording that you think people will find fascinating, you can go to a freelancer marketplace such as Elance, Guru, ODesk or others and hire a writer, video creator, voiceover artist, web designer or other skilled professional to create your content for you. Even if you don't already have an original idea, you can usually work with a freelance to develop something collaboratively, or have them handle it all for you from start to finish.

Using a freelancer marketplace is beneficial because the site will normally handle all billing, payment and dispute arbitration so you don't have to worry about any of that. They also take care of all the licensing and copyright agreements so that you don't have to worry about authorship issues or somebody suing you for copyright infringement later.

The benefit of hiring a freelancer is that they can provide high-quality content without much input or direction from you, usually at surprisingly affordable prices. And once they submit their creation to you and are paid, it belongs entirely to you and you can do with it whatever you please without having to pay royalties, residuals or any additional payments.

A third option is to use Private Label Rights products. These are eBooks, videos, software and other content that already has been created by somebody else that you can purchase and resell it as your very own under your own name or brand.

Depending on the terms of the purchase, usually you can claim original authorship if you choose. Or you can add new content, remove parts of it, or edit it any way you like. You also can combine multiple PLR products to create a new product or take a single PLR product and split it up into multiple products that you can either give away or sell. Some PLR products even allow you to resell the rights to resell them as your PLR products to other marketers.

While there are hundreds of places where you can purchase PLR products, among the best sources are:

- UnstopppablePLR

- UnselfishMarketer

The benefit of PLR products is that they are available in practically every niche, so you can get high-quality content that you can either give away as a LMR or promote as an original product to your subscribers. They usually are very affordable as well.

Building Your First List

To create your first subscriber list, you will need to start with an email account. You probably don't want to use your personal account because it might become too difficult to manage both your personal communications and interactions with subscribers. So you should consider opening a new account with one of the big email providers, such as Gmail or Yahoo.

If your business already has a name you should use this as the name on your new email account if it is available. If you don't have a business name or your name isn't available, try to pick something related to the niche you will be working in, for example LoseWeightFast@gmail.com or DiscountSportsMemorabilia@yahoo.com.

Next you will need a website called an opt-in page that will serve as an entry point for your prospective subscribers. An opt-in page can be your squeeze page – in which you give away your LMR – or it can simply be a place for visitors to opt-in to your business or service, such as contacting you for a free consultation or setting up a doctor's appointment.

If you have never built a website before, it can seem intimidating. But you no longer need to be an expert on writing code or have a degree in web design in order to make a great-looking high-converting website. There are plenty of free tools you can use to set up a website in just a few minutes.

One of the best is WordPress. This is an open source site that you can use to build a website for free using their simple online tools, many of which are drag-and-drop. WordPress has existing free and paid templates that you can use to simply add your new content and have a great-looking website. Or you can build an entirely new website on your own using their free tools.

Another option is to hire somebody to build your website for you. There are many companies that specialize in these types of projects, but they can be costly. You also can hire a freelancer from one of the marketplaces mentioned earlier, which is often a more affordable option.

Regardless of whether you build it yourself or hire somebody to create your website, you will need a domain name and a hosting service.

A domain name is going to be the URL address of your website. In other words, it's going to be the link to where visitors can find it, for example www.CutePuppies4Sale.com or www.GreatBooksDiscussionGroup.org.

There are lots of sites where you can purchase a domain name. Usually you buy it for a period of time, such as a year or 24 months. Although the cost depends on which site you use, what offers they have, and how long your lease it, generally you can expect to pay anywhere from $9 to $29/year per domain name.

Once you have a domain name, you will need to lease space on a server to host your site. Again, there are many different companies that specialize in hosting websites. Costs tend to range from about $99 to $199/year, depending on the size and level of service you require. Once you sign up, simply follow the online instructions to link your new domain name to your hosting service.

Once you have built your opt-in page (or had it built for you), WordPress will ask you to input your domain name as the URL for your new website. When you do this, whenever anybody types in that address, they will be directed to your website.

Finally, you want to load your LMR into your autoresponder and connect autoresponder to your website. Then, whenever visitors arrive on your page and opt-in by giving you their email address, your autoresponder will automatically take care of sending out your free lead magnet and adding their email to your subscription list.

If you LMR is something people passionate about your niche are going to want to have your subscription list will quickly fill up with hundreds or even thousands of new highly-targeted subscribers who have already proven that they are interested in the types of products and service you are promoting.

Traffic: How to Populate Your List

The key to any successful online marketing program is to get as much traffic as possible to your website. As long as you are giving away a high-value product for free, you are going to capture a high percentage of visitors. This is known as a visitor conversion because you are converting visitors into subscribers once they opt-in to your list.

Traffic can be divided into two types: Paid and free.

Paid traffic methods include buying ad on Google, Facebook and other popular ad providers; buying banner ads that appear on the top, sides and bottom of popular websites related to your niche; buying lists of subscribers from other Internet marketers; and many other options.

Free traffic marketing includes using social media to attract people who are interested in your niche to visit your website; participating in niche-related discussions in chat rooms, forum, social media pages and other locations and encouraging people to visit your website; creating a blog and writing regularly about your niche topic and including a link to your website; and many other free methods.

If you are just starting out, you can use free traffic methods until you build your list so large that it starts to attract a lot of prospective customers so you can start building revenues. Then you can reinvest some or all of these revenues into paid traffic methods so that you can build your list even more quickly.

Obviously, free traffic methods take a lot longer to gain traction. It can take weeks or even months before you start to get the kind of response that is going to provide you with enough revenues to fund your paid traffic marketing.

Paid traffic, on the other hand, can provide traffic almost instantly. With such popular platforms as Facebook Ads or Google Ads, you can get your ads in front of highly-targeted prospects right away, so it's not unusual for you to start getting visitors to your site almost moments after you launch your paid traffic platforms.

Not all traffic generation methods are created equal. Some work better than others and will bring you results more quickly. The fastest and most cost-effective traffic generation methods are:

1. Joint Ventures (Paid)

2. Pay-Per-Click, Pay-Per-View and Banner Ads (Paid)

3. Social Media/Blogging (Free)

4. Forums, Ad Swaps and Safelists (Free/Paid)

Joint ventures are when you enter into an agreement with another marketer – usually somebody who already works within your niche – and agree to share the costs of promotion equally. Both parties promote the business to their own lists and profits are then split down the middle. Joint ventures are a great way to get twice the mileage out of your promotional budget for half the cost. Joint venture partners can be found in many different places online, but one of the best and easiest to use is Warrior Forum, a site that specializes in bringing Internet marketers together.

When you buy PPC, PPV or banner ads, you deal with an external ad broker, such as Facebook Ads or Google AdWords, and pay to have ads sent to high-target web users. With PPC, you pay only for those who click through to your pages. With PPV and banner ads, you pay for a certain number of impressions, or pages on which your ad will appear.

Ad swaps are another helpful way to expand your list quickly. It's when you agree to trade lists with another marketer. You send out emails to their list promoting your web page and they send your subscribers a link to their page. It's a fast and free way to double your exposure. Potential ad swap partners can be found at Warrior Forum and many other Internet marketing exchange sites.

Solo ads are when you pay another marketer to promote your link to their subscribers, usually in the form of a recommendation in an email or in a newsletter. For as little as $10 you can buy solo ads that include links back to your squeeze pages, opt-in pages or websites.

Email Swipes

Once you have a list of subscribers who have already proven they are passionate about your niche, the next step is to set up a series of emails – called email swipes -- that you program your autoresponder to send out according to a pre-set schedule. There is no limit to the number of emails you can send out and your subscriber will keep receiving them from you until they unsubscribe.

The emails you send out should serve one of two purposes:

1. To reinforce the loyalty bond your subscriber has to you by giving them something of high value for free

2. To promote a particular product or service

An effective email swipe series will contain both types of emails. If you only send out emails that are promoting products and services, it's unlikely that your subscribers are going to take a lot of value from your emails and they will be more likely to unsubscribe faster.

But if you alternate these promotional emails with others in which you provide free high-value content that they can actually use in their everyday lives, then your subscribers will be more likely to open your emails when you send them and will be more open to purchasing the products or services you promote when you send promotional emails.

Free high-value emails can contain original content that you have developed yourself or purchased in the form of freelancer content, PLR or some other source. Or they can simply contain links to informative content you have found that you know your subscribers will find useful.

It's helpful if you think of your emails swipes as a newsletter that you are sending your subscribers. When you get a newsletter, you expect it to contain interesting and helpful articles about topics that you are interested in. If the content is high quality and you enjoy reading it, you are going to be more open to buying the products and services that are promoted in that newsletter.

Although there is no agreed-upon schedule for free content/promotional emails, you probably will want to use at least a 3:1 proportion: For every promotional email you send out, you send out three in which you simply provide free high value content designed to cement loyalty bonds between your subscribers and you.

When it comes time to send out a promotional email, it should take a structure that is similar to a sales letter in that it has a clear Call to Action (CTA). This is what exactly you want your reader to do: Buy a product, subscribe to a newsletter, invest in your company, etc.

For example, if you are promoting an eBook on fly fishing to ardent fishermen, everything in your promotional email should be geared toward showing how valuable and useful that eBook is, why you recommend it, and encouraging your subscribers to buy it now.

Promotional emails also must include a link to where your subscribers can go to buy the products or services you are promoting.

A word on products and services: Like your LMR, the content you promote in your promotional videos can be either original or something you paid somebody else to create for you. A third option, however, is to promote affiliate products. These are products that are sold by somebody else but promoted by you. Anytime one of your subscribers clicks through and purchases one of these affiliate products, you get paid a commission on the sale.

Affiliate products are probably the popular type of promotions among email marketers. That's because they don't require you to purchase anything up front, carry any inventory, or even worry about delivering the product to the buyer. All you need to do is promote the product and when a sale is made, you get paid.

There are literally thousands of affiliate products you can promote in practically every niche imaginable. If you promote physical products, Amazon has one of the largest and most successful affiliate programs anywhere. If you are promoting digital products – such as eBooks, videos, software and so on – Clickbank is one of the biggest digital affiliate product sources.

Making Money with Your Email List

When you have developed a list of loyal subscribers and have provided them with lots of free high-value content, they will absolutely be looking forward to your emails. They are also highly likely to act on your offers and rewards.

The first offer you make is called the gateway offer. This should be a really great niche-related product that you are offering at an amazingly low price. The purpose of the gateway offer is not to make a short-term profit. In fact, you should consider offering your gateway offer at break-even cost or even at a loss. That's because the gateway offer is all about winning the long-term loyalty of your customers.

When you provide your subscribers with true value, you can cement long-term trust bonds and keep them buying whatever you are selling for months, or even years, to come.

Making sure you alternate your promotional emails with those that offer free high-value content, links and other trust-builders, you can next provide secondary offers. These should be a series of increasingly expensive niche-related products and services. These series of products that have higher and higher price tags are known as the profit ladder.

The stronger the trust bonds you can build with your customers, the further you can push them up the profit ladder. For example, if your niche is dating and relationships and your gateway offer is an eBook priced at $5, your first secondary offer could be a video course that sells in the $19 to $25 range. Next you can offer one or two products in the $95 to $200 range. Once you really have established a solid relationship with your subscribers, you can offer even higher priced offers, in the $500 to $1,000 range.

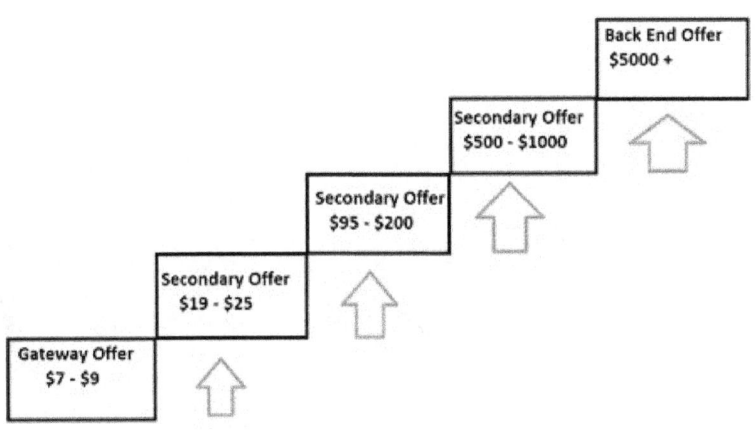

Finally, you can offer what's known as your back end offer. This is something that carries a truly high price tag, such as a $5,000 weekend-long boot camp at an exclusive spa resort. While very few of your subscribers will make it all the way up your profit ladder to the back end offer, you only need a few people to buy it in order to make a huge profit.

EZ List Building

While it may seem intimidating to newcomers, thanks to technological advances and streamlining of coding and programming, building and launching a website today is actually quite simple.

Once you use your website to create your first list of subscribers and experience the loading your autoresponder with email swipes in which you alternate informational and promotional emails in order to push your subscribers up the profit ladder, doing it a second or third time will be even easier.

These list building techniques can be used to promote products or services – either your own or somebody else's – or simply to connect with other people who share your interests. If you are a small business owner, you can use them to build customer loyalty and expand your customer base.

The best part about list building is that once you master the basics, it becomes very easy to manage and maintain. You can literally set it and forget it. As new prospects discover your opt-in page and give you their email address, your autoresponder can take care of 95% of the rest of the process of moving them up the profit ladder and bringing you a steady, reliable and essentially hands-free income stream. That's what makes EZ List Building so attractive to Internet marketers.

Good luck!